NANA'S LIFE STORY

Preserve Nana's most meaningful moments and memories in this Guided Life Story Keepsake Journal.

Her Memories. Her Love. Your Heirloom

Capturing stories of those you love the most
www.memwah.com.au

This journal is dedicated to my Nana Helen, her stories untold, the laughter shared, and the profound legacy she has left behind. I now share with my daughters your tales of strength, your grace, and the mysteries that made you uniquely you.

With all my love. Tam x

Grandma's Life Story Journal
©2024 by Tammie Winward, Founder of Memwah. All rights reserved.
Published by Memwah Publishing
Melbourne, Australia
www.memwah.com.au
Scan the QR code below to find out more about Memwah

Cover design by Whiteseed Collective
https://whiteseedcollective.com/
Cover image credit Gojak
ISBN: 978-1-7635267-6-1

First Edition: March 2024

No part of this book may be used or reproduced in any manner whatsoever without written permission except in the case of brief quotations embodied in critical articles and reviews.

Contact: support@memwah.com.au

THIS BOOK IS TO BE PASSED DOWN TO:

Name
_____

Message
_____
_____
_____
_____
_____
_____

How well do you know your parents and grandparents, like really know them? What are their most treasured memories? What makes them happy? How do they feel about the state of the world?

Don't know the answers? You're not the only one. Many people say that it wasn't until their parents passed away that they realized how little they knew about them – and by then it was too late.

Everyone has a story to tell, even your parents. And as you get older, your parents' stories will become even more precious because, ultimately, it's memories that they'll leave behind.

So how do you get to know your parents and hear their stories? You ask them questions.

I'm Tammie Winward, the founder of Memwah, which is a Life Story Video Maker. I'm on a mission to save a generation of stories. My mother-in-law Jenny had a story to tell, and it was her story that started this journey to help families capture and preserve their stories.

Jenny had always wanted to write her life stories and share them with her grandchildren. But her dream of becoming a writer had passed years ago, and the task of putting pen to paper was now overwhelming.

Jenny's 70th birthday was coming up. I wanted to give her something momentous. I thought, what better birthday gift than to help Jenny write her life story? So I hired a writer who would sit with her while she recounted her favorite memories. The writer recorded it, transcribed it, and edited it into a book.

I felt deeply moved as I sat with Jenny and listened to her recount her life. I thought, what a privilege to listen to another person's life story. I learned more about my husband Lukas and received a deeper understanding of what led him to become the wonderful man he is today.

Together, we found things out about Jenny we would never have known if we hadn't asked a writer to help us. It was an experience I'll remember forever.

Soon after Jenny's birthday, I fell pregnant. When my beautiful baby girl Maggie was born, she was put on life support for 10 months. While sitting in the hospital day after day, worrying about my baby's health, I reflected on what was important in life.

Why are we here? What does it all mean? It got pretty existential, I have to admit! I thought about what's most important to me. I realized it's the people I love most and the stories we share. This realization led to another one. There were many things I had never asked my parents, like how my grandfather died or how my dad felt about coming home after the Vietnam War.

So after 22 years working as an Events Producer, I decided I wanted to do something else. I wanted to ask the important questions. How could I make documenting life stories easy? How could I encourage others to share their memories with the people they loved most? How could I make it easy, accessible, and affordable so anyone could do it?

And so, Memwah was born. A Life Story Video Maker that prompts you with thought-provoking questions, records your answers and compiles them into a memorable video for you to share.

Along the way I've learned that capturing your life story is a personal journey. Some are drawn to writing, whilst others are not writers and prefer the ease of creating a video memoir. I've designed this journal to support either method. With 100 prompts to guide your memories, you can find inspiration to fill the pages with your stories.

For those intrigued by the idea of video, the journal serves as a gentle introduction. Creating a video memoir ensures your family never forgets your voice, your laugh or that story. If this is your style then start with the journal, use it to gather thoughts and memories, and then, when you're ready, use those notes as a foundation for your Life Story Video on Memwah.

We all carry stories. Each and every one of our stories is precious and deserves to be heard – yes, even the embarrassing stories you'd rather forget!

Lastly, we're a small Australian business and are committed to helping families be able to make their memories last forever. Your support and feedback are so important to us as it's through your **reviews, comments and emails** that we can tell if we are on the right track.

Why did you create a story and what impact did it have on you and your friends and family? We would love to hear from you.

With stories and memories,

Tam.

Scan here to leave a review

HOW TO USE THIS JOURNAL

- Embrace Your Unique Story: Your life story is uniquely yours. As you approach this journal, remember that every life is a blend of triumphs and trials, happiness and heartache. Be honest and authentic in your reflections.
- No Pressure for Perfection: Perfection is not the goal. Your thoughts, memories, and reflections, no matter how they are expressed, are valuable. This journal is a place for raw, unfiltered expression. Spelling mistakes, crossed-out words, and messy handwriting are all part of the process.
- Choose What Resonates: Not every prompt in this journal may resonate with your personal experiences or life story. If you come across a prompt that doesn't seem relevant, feel free to make it your own. You can cross it out, cover it with white label stickers, or simply write your own question or topic over the top. This journal is a space for your unique story, so tailor it to fit you perfectly.

Tips for Journaling

- Take Your Time: Don't feel pressured to complete the journal quickly. You might find some days are more conducive to reflection than others. Let your journey through this journal unfold naturally.
- Mix and Match: Feel free to answer questions out of order. You might start with a prompt from the middle of the journal that speaks to you and later return to earlier questions. Your story doesn't have to be linear.
- Add Your Personality: Use the empty pages at the back of the journal to add anything you feel is missing. You can include additional memories, paste in photos, draw, or even jot down quotes or poems that are meaningful to you.
- Be Brave: Some prompts might encourage you to dig deep into your experiences and emotions. Be brave in facing these reflections. The act of writing can be incredibly therapeutic and insightful.
- Share (If You Wish): If you feel comfortable, sharing your story or parts of it with loved ones can be a powerful experience. But never feel obligated to share anything you wish to keep private.

Your life story journal is more than just a collection of pages; it's a reflection of your journey, a testament to your resilience, and a celebration of your achievements. As you fill these pages, remember that life is an ongoing story. There will always be more to add, more to reflect on, and more to learn.

Take this journey one page at a time, and remember, the beauty of your story lies in its authenticity.

Need more space? Jump onto www.memwah.com.au and record your answers. Don't let a single detail go untold—capture it all on video.

I read of a man who stood to speak at a funeral of a friend. He referred to the dates on the tombstone from the beginning...to the end.

He noted that first came the date of birth and spoke of the following date with tears but said what mattered most of all was the dash between those years.

For that dash represents all the time they spent alive on earth and now only those who loved them know what that little line is worth.

For it matters not, how much we own, the cars...the house...the cash. What matters is how we lived and loved and how we spend our dash.

So, think about this long and hard; are there things you'd like to change? For you never know how much time is left that still can be rearranged.

To be less quick to anger and show appreciation more
and love the people in our lives like we've never loved before.
If we treat each other with respect and more often wear a smile...
remembering that this special dash might only last a little while.

So, when your eulogy is being read, with your life's actions to rehash, would you be proud of the things they say about how you lived your dash?

———————————————

Linda Ellis

THE CONTENT

- 1   LIFE STORIES
- 2   MEMORY LANE
- 10   PROCESS OVER PRODUCT
- 14   ABOUT ME
- 20   THE EARLY YEARS
- 41   CAREER, TRAVEL AND LIFE EXPERIENCES
- 50   PARENTHOOD
- 63   CULTURE AND BELIEFS
- 74   LOVE
- 93   FINAL REFLECTIONS
- 114   YOUR QUESTIONS AND NOTES
- 121   THANK YOU

LIFE STORIES

Documenting your life stories and creating your memoir is a powerful way to create a legacy for your loved ones. Whether it's writing down your memories, recording life stories on audio or video, or simply sharing your stories with your family and friends, preserving your life stories can have a lasting impact on generations to come.

During the pandemic, I designed a Life Story Video Maker called Memwah as a way for my children to connect with their grandparents. I was concerned that my parents were not getting any younger and I wanted to preserve their stories for myself and also my children. Unfortunately, unlike you, my parents were not writers so I needed to find a way to capture their story easily which is why I thought video would be a great tool.

While building Memwah and engaging with storytellers, I discovered the profound impact of capturing personal stories—it's our way of showing our loved ones they truly matter. This realization has set me on a mission to capture a generation of stories, including yours.

Imagine a world where every primary school student studying their family tree can ask their grandparents a question and record it, and every person entering an aged care facility has the opportunity to share who they are, what they've learned in life, and how they wish to be remembered, preserving a wealth of lives and experiences for posterity.

You've paid for insurance your whole life, so why not ensure that your life and your memories are captured, saved, and shared with your family and friends?

Reflecting and sharing your life story is a gift not only to your loved ones but also to yourself. Your stories are important and help shape your loved one's worldview, giving them insight, shared knowledge and wisdom.

Regardless of how you do it, you are important, your story is important and sharing and compiling your story will be a legacy to loved ones that they will cherish forever.

MEMORY LANE

Worried you won't remember past events? You're not alone! As we age, our memories get a little fuzzy. Think of your brain as a storage unit. It absorbs copious amounts of data every day and catalogs it depending on the type of memory – sensory, short-term, or long-term.

Long-term memory is like getting old boxes out from the back – it requires a bit of effort! The best thing about this process is through the art of storytelling, you can unlock long-term memories and share these stories with your loved ones!

LET YOUR SENSES EVOKE EMOTION

Has a smell ever transported you back to your childhood? Or a taste reminded you of a past event? Your brain stores sense memories. This is why sights, sounds, smells, and tastes can evoke emotional memories you may have forgotten.

If you have or think you will have a strong emotional reaction to a sight, sound, taste, or smell, revisit it and see what happens. Cook a meal your Mom used to make when you were a child or play a song you loved when you were a teenager.

When you feel an emotion, instead of feeling the feeling and moving on, sit with it and write down your memories. You'll be surprised at what comes up.

TIPS TO OPEN UP YOUR SENSES

On the worksheet following, write a list of meals you could cook, music and items from your past for you to explore and evoke nostalgia.

Examples below:
- Cook your favorite meal from when you were a child
- Drive down the street where you grew up or visit some of your old haunts.
- Create playlists of songs from different periods of your life and listen to them. Each song can transport you back to specific Moments, feelings, and experiences.
- Look up the news headlines from the year you were 18
- Read old letters, journals, or emails
- Pull out the old projector, play old family videos, and look through your family photo albums.

MEMORY LANE

YOUR SENSES

- [ ]
- [ ]
- [ ]
- [ ]
- [ ]
- [ ]
- [ ]
- [ ]
- [ ]
- [ ]
- [ ]
- [ ]
- [ ]
- [ ]
- [ ]

MEMORY LANE

It's true that as we age, our memories fade, but it doesn't mean they're forgotten forever. Memory cues help us remember.

An example of this is when an old friend or family member recalls an event and you remember details you didn't remember before. Their experience acts as a memory cue, which unlocks your experience of the event.

You can make your own memory cues with this simple exercise.

- For each five-year increment, write down the big events you remember, e.g. starting primary school.
- Write down the most meaningful events and try and fill in the details. These will inspire you with stories to tell.

MAJOR EVENTS

0- 5	
5-10	
10-15	
15 - 20	

MEMORY LANE

20 - 25		
25 - 30		
30 - 35		
35 - 40		
40 - 45		
45 - 50		
50 - 55		

MEMORY LANE

55 - 60		
60 - 65		
65 - 70		
70 - 75		
75 - 80		
85 - 90		
90 - 100		

MEMORY LANE

WHERE WERE YOU WHEN....
HAPPENED

Event	Where were you and how did it make you feel?
Assassination of John F. Kennedy - 22 November 1963	
Moon Landing - 21 July, 1969	
John Lennon is Assassinated - 8 December 1980	
Fall of the Berlin Wall - 9 November 1989	
Death of Diana, Princess of Wales - 31 August 1997	
9/11 terrorist attacks - 11 September 2001	
Death of Queen Elizabeth II - 8 September 2022	

CONNECT WITH OLD FAMILY AND FRIENDS

Your memory is subjective. An event will differ greatly from someone else's. Use this to your advantage.

Get in touch with a friend or family member you spent considerable time with in the era you're trying to remember. Ask them open-ended questions – questions that start with "What" "How" and "Why".

Conversations about the "old times" almost always lead to memory retrieval. Much like talk therapy, talking about your memories helps you refine the ones you do remember, and remember the ones you don't.

MEMORY LANE

LIST OUT OLD FRIENDS FROM THE PAST

NAME	EMAIL	PHONE

Notes

PROCESS OVER PRODUCT

Each memory, no matter how seemingly trivial, is a thread in the intricate tapestry of your life. By pulling on these threads, you not only recall your past but also reconnect with the emotions, challenges, and triumphs that have shaped you. This process is not a linear path but a winding road, filled with discoveries and revelations at every turn.

Focusing on the process rather than the final product shifts your perspective, making the act of journaling an end in itself. Remember, this journal is not meant to be a polished manuscript or a showcase of penmanship. Its true value lies in its authenticity. Don't worry about your handwriting, after all like life, it can be messy.

Not all the question prompts will be relevant to you. Feel free to leave a question blank, cross it out, or add your questions to the blank pages on the back. This is your story. Start where you are, use what you have, and do what you can.

PROCESS

INTENTIONS

Storytelling

- What draws you to write your life story or family history now?
- Is there a specific event, realization, or inspiration that sparked this desire?

What are your goals?

- What do you hope to achieve by documenting your life story or family history?
- Are you seeking healing, understanding, preservation of memory, connecting with future generations, or something else?

Audience

- Who are you writing for? Yourself, your family, a broader audience?
- How does your intended audience influence what and how you choose to write?

Anticipating obstacles

- What challenges do you anticipate facing as you embark on this storytelling journey (e.g. emotional distress, writer's block, lack of information)?

- How can you prepare for and address these challenges?

Support Systems

We have found that reflecting on the past can bring up serious emotions both positive and some that can be challenging. If you feel that you need to explore these feelings further or need someone to talk to, we recommend seeking support.

- Who or what could support you in this journey (e.g. family members, writing groups, historical research, therapists)?

Commitment

Can you create a simple ritual or choose a symbol to remind you of your intentions and motivations throughout this process?

- Example: Lighting a candle before each writing session or wearing a special piece of jewellery as a symbol of your commitment.

Writing Your Intention Statement

Craft a detailed intention statement incorporating your reflections, goals, and how you plan to honor this commitment.

- Example: "I commit to exploring and documenting my family's values and history focusing on the themes of resilience and love. I will approach challenges with patience and seek support when needed, always remembering that this journey is a gift to myself and future generations."

First step

- What is one small, manageable step you can take today or this week to begin your storytelling journey?

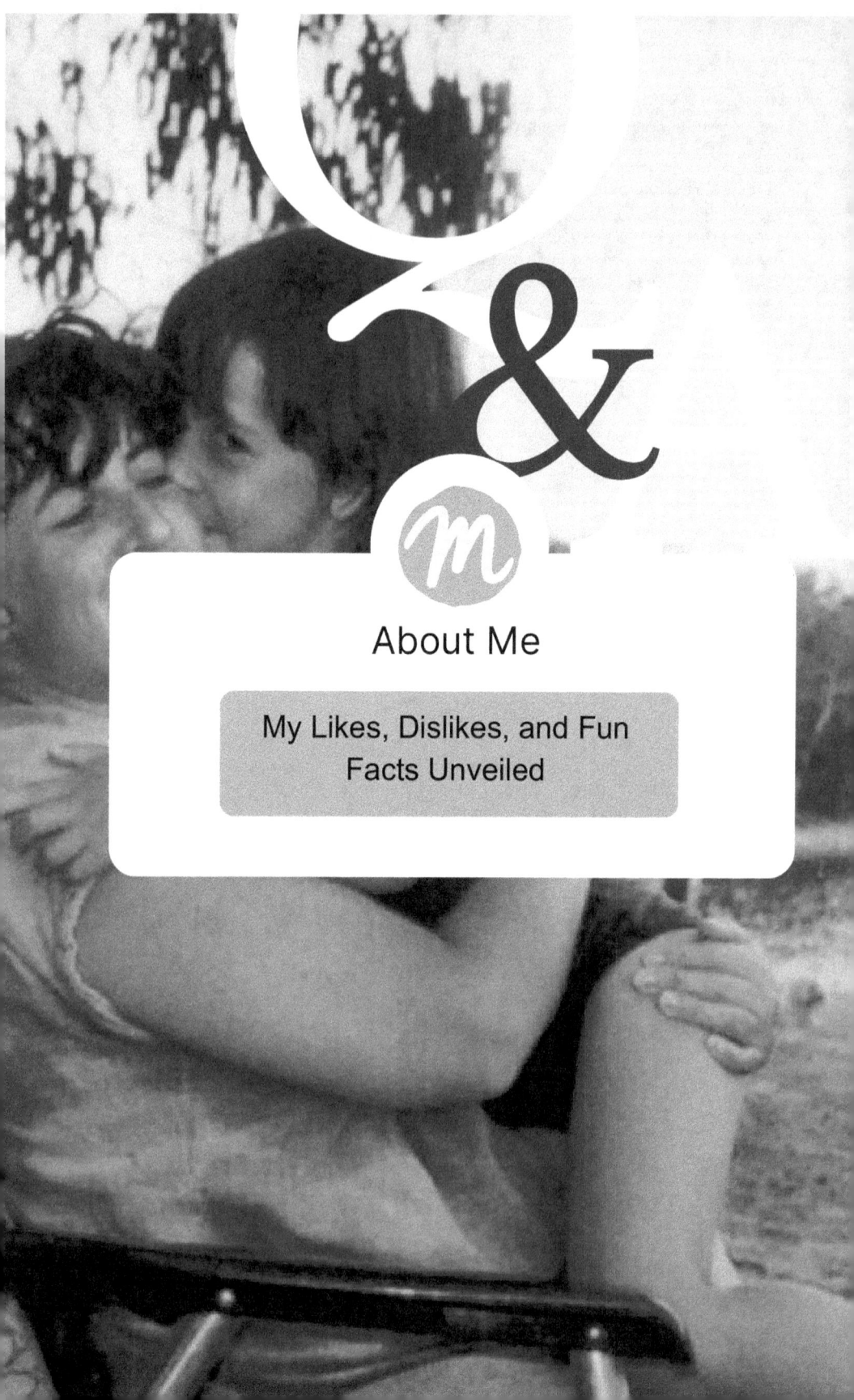

About Me

My Likes, Dislikes, and Fun Facts Unveiled

ABOUT ME

Paste a photo here

My name is:

Other names:

Nicknames:

Date when you started this journal:

D.O.B: Hospital:

Parents name:

Weight at birth:

Blood type:

Shoe size:

Height:

Places I have lived:

My first word was:

My siblings are:

Describe your personality:

How would others would describe you?

Top 3 Values

01   02   03

FUN FACTS

- What is your favorite meal?

....

- Are you a dog or a cat person?

....

- What is your favorite movie?

....

- Have you ever broken any bones?

....

- Do you prefer the cold or the heat?

....

- What sport(s) do you follow and who is your team?

....

- What's an unexpected talent you have that would surprise everyone? Describe the first time you discovered or showcased this talent.

....

....

....

- Are you a morning person or a night owl?

- Whats the one thing you've done that you never thought you would do?

- If you could relive one year of your life which would it be and why?

- What are you really good at?

- What fashion trend have you loved the most?

- What's a small thing that disproportionately annoys you?

Your Space: Write down some interesting facts about yourself

The bad news is time flies. The good news is you're the pilot.

Micheal Altshuler

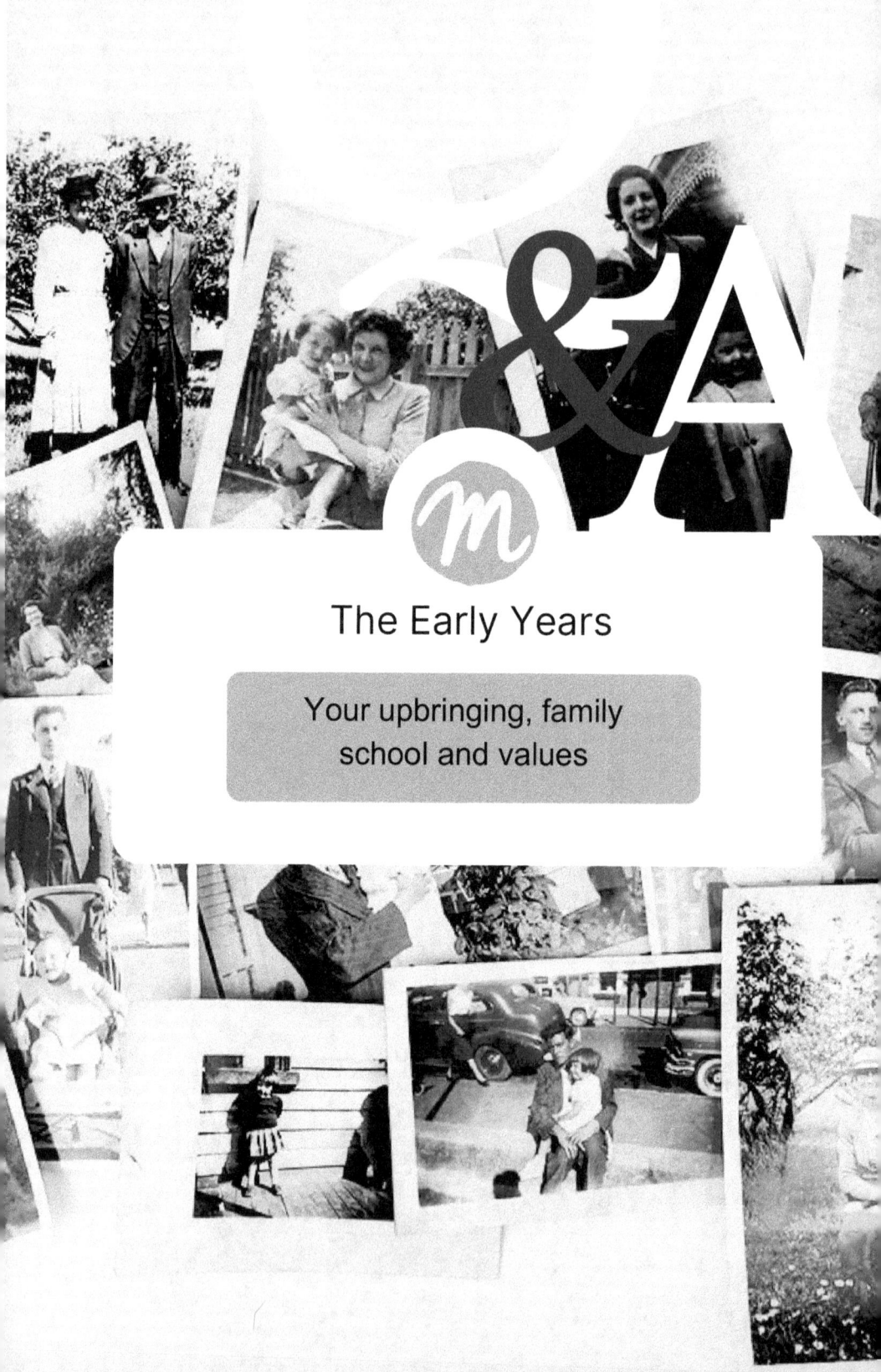

The Early Years

Your upbringing, family school and values

ⓜ What is your name and what is the story behind it?

....

....

....

....

....

....

....

....

....

....

ⓜ Have you ever changed your name and how did you come to that decision?

....

....

....

....

....

....

ⓜ Describe your childhood home...

....

....

....

....

....

....

....

ⓜ What is your earliest memory?

....

....

....

....

....

....

....

If at first you don't succeed, try doing it the way your Mom told you to do it from the start.

———————————

Unknown

Describe your Mom...

Describe your Dad...

💗 What was your relationship like with your parents?

💗 What was your relationship like with your grandparents?

♡ What is your earliest memory of your parents, and how does it reflect the overall nature of your relationship with them? Describe the emotions, sights, and sounds

♡ Think about the core values and beliefs your parents instilled in you. Which of these have you carried into your life, and how have they shaped the person you've become?

Reflect on a significant challenge your family faced together. How did your parents handle the situation, and what did you learn from their response to adversity?

As you grew older, how did your relationship with your parents evolve? Identify a pivotal moment when you saw them in a different light, and describe how that moment affected your relationship.

💗 Did you have any siblings and if so, who are they and what is / was your relationship like with them?

_____
_____
_____
_____
_____
_____
_____

💗 How has your relationship with your sibling(s) evolved from childhood through adulthood? Discuss any pivotal events or phases that significantly altered your dynamic, and how you navigated these changes together or apart.

_____
_____
_____
_____
_____
_____
_____

💬 Describe your summer holidays when you were growing up?

💬 Did you have any health problems growing up?

m What was life like before the internet?

m What are the catchphrases or sayings you're most known for among friends and family? For example, have you ever quipped, 'We're not going to a fashion show,' to hurry things along? Share those signature lines and the stories behind them.

SCHOOL DAYS

ⓜ What school(s) did you go to?

....
....
....
....

ⓜ What subject did you excel in at school?

....

ⓜ What was your go-to meal or snack during school lunchtime?

....

ⓜ Were you part of any clubs, teams, or organizations at school? What role did you play?

....
....

ⓜ Did you receive any awards or special recognition during your school years? What were they for?

....
....
....

💬 Who was your favorite teacher and what impact did they have on you?

....
....
....
....
....
....
....

💬 Who was your best friend when you were young? What was your favourite thing to do together?

....
....
....
....
....
....
....
....
....

m Did you ever get in trouble when you were young? Sent to the principal's office? How did you navigate your rebellious years?

....
....
....
....
....
....
....
....
....
....

m How does growing up today differ from when you were a young?

....
....
....
....
....
....

m Who were your role models growing up and what values did you learn from them?

....
....
....
....
....
....
....

m Describe a time when you were afraid...

....
....
....
....
....
....
....

Think about someone from your past who you miss the most. What would you say to them if you could? Write them a letter here, sharing your thoughts and feelings.

If you could reach back through time, what advice, wisdom, or words of support would you offer to your younger self? Write a letter here to the person you were, acknowledging the challenges faced and celebrating the growth achieved.

Your Space: Thoughts and Memories

....

....

....

....

....

....

....

....

....

Date of the photo ....

I've always likened the creation of my life to weaving a tapestry, with every choice of material, subject, and color lying within my grasp.

As I weave, a stunning image unfolds on the front, concealing the chaos of dropped stitches and tangled threads—representing confusion and doubt—on the back.

In moments of struggle or failure, I often find myself fixated on this disarray, failing to see any coherent design.

Yet, with time and wisdom, I've come to understand that a beautiful pattern is indeed taking shape on the other side. It's a reminder to shift my focus and appreciate the masterpiece of life as it's being crafted.

Jennifer Winward - My Mother-In-Law who is one of the best storytellers I know

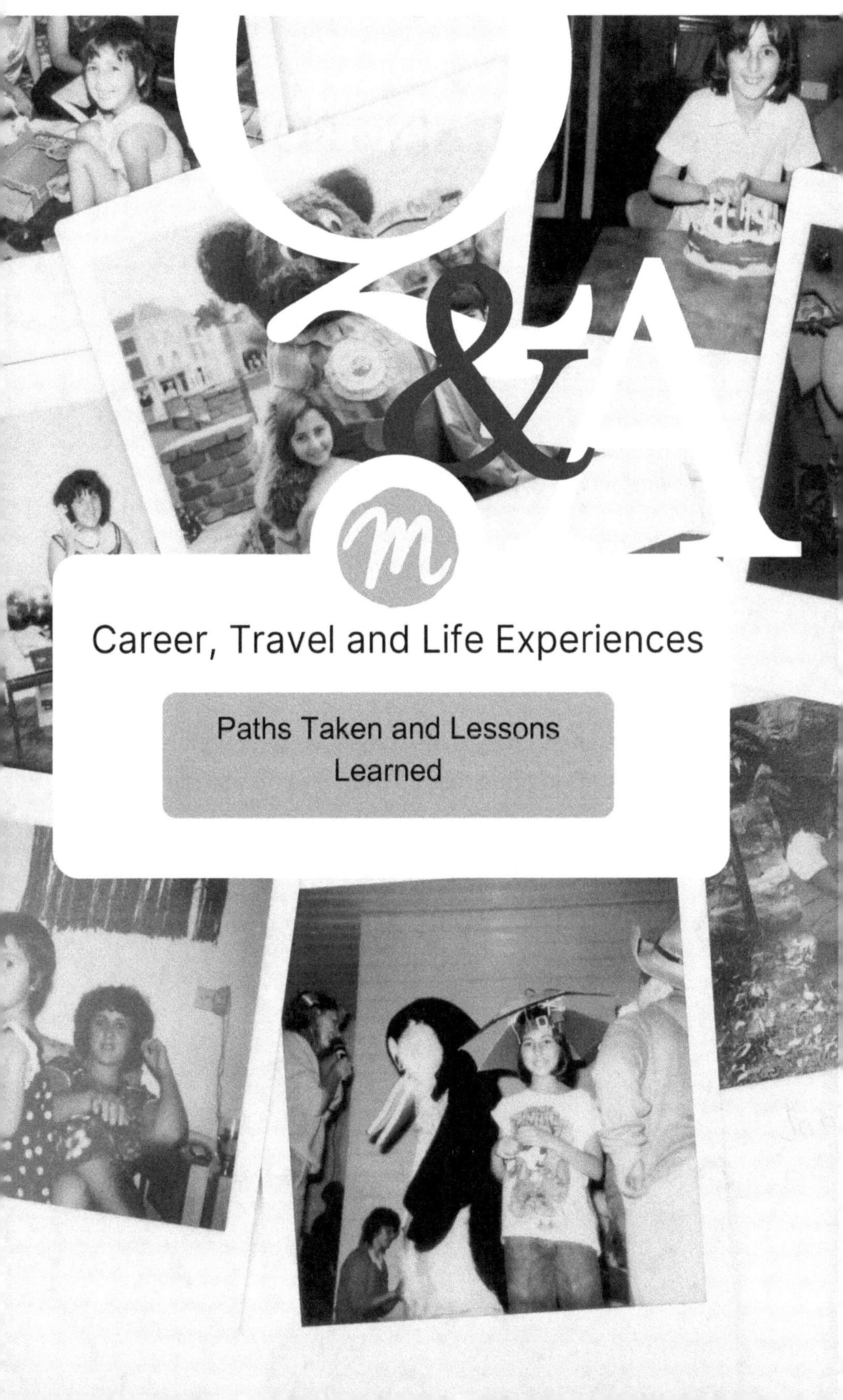

Q&A

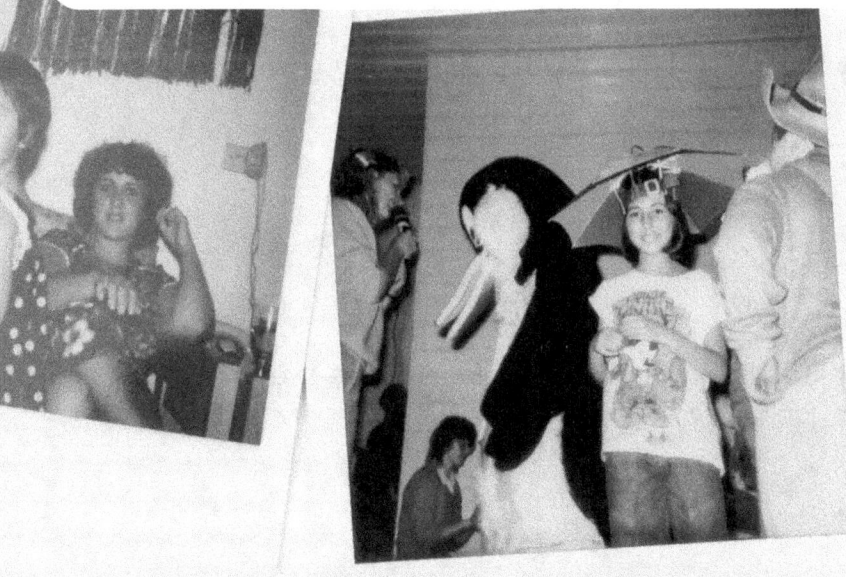

Career, Travel and Life Experiences

Paths Taken and Lessons Learned

LIGHTNING ROUND

- What languages do you speak?

- If you could time-travel to any destination at any point in history, where and when would you go?

- Window or Aisle?

- What is your favorite season?

- What's one song you secretly love but might not admit to liking in public? When do you usually listen to it?

- What is the biggest invention or innovation you've witnessed in your lifetime?

- What's the most unusual food you've ever tasted?

Reflect on your very first job. What was it, how did you spend your first paycheck and what valuable lessons did you learn that have stayed with you?

....

....

....

....

....

....

....

List out the jobs / roles you have had across your life

Comapny	Role	Year started	Year ended

m Throughout your career and life, which position or role have you found the most joy in, and why?

_____
_____
_____
_____
_____

m Have you ever quit on the spot and what happened next?

_____
_____
_____
_____
_____

m If you could've chosen a different career, what other pathway might you have pursued?

_____
_____
_____
_____

🅜 Share the achievement in your career or life that you are most proud of. Why does this particular achievement stand out to you?

....
....
....
....
....

🅜 What was one of the biggest challenges you faced in your career or role, and how did you overcome it?

....
....
....
....
....

🅜 Do you live to work or work to live?

....
....
....
....
....
....

💬 How has your industry or field changed during the time you've been a part of it? What do you think these changes say about the future of your profession?

....

....

....

....

....

....

....

💬 Reflect on a significant "fork in the road" moment in your life. What were the options, and how did you make your decision? Looking back, how has this choice shaped your journey?

....

....

....

....

....

....

....

💬 Reflect on a trip that has had a significant impact on you. What made this travel experience memorable?

_____
_____
_____
_____
_____

💬 Where have you travelled, what has been your favorite destination?

_____
_____
_____
_____

💬 Share a moment from your travels when you experienced a striking cultural difference. Was it a mishap, an observation, or perhaps a language barrier that led to an unexpected adventure or insight?

_____
_____
_____
_____

BUCKET LIST DESTINATIONS

Where does your heart long to roam? List out the places you've always dreamed of exploring

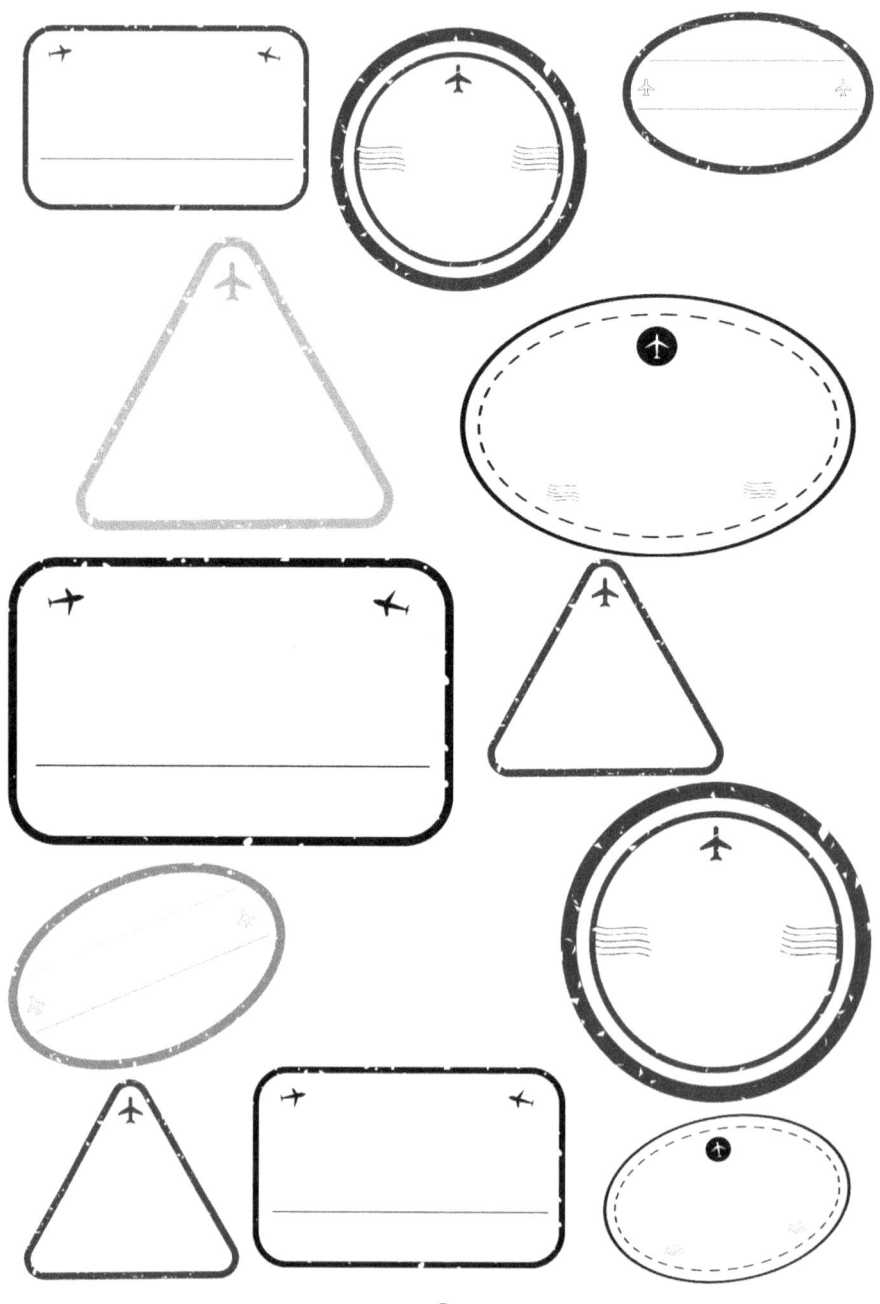

Your Space: Thoughts and Memories

....

....

....

....

....

....

....

....

Stick a holiday photo here

Date of the photo ....

Q&A

Parenthood

Family, Parenting, Grandparents and Celebrating Every Journey

🤍 Describe the moment when you first realized you were going to be a parent. What were your initial thoughts and feelings?

....

....

....

....

....

....

....

....

🤍 How do you think becoming a Mom has changed you as a person?

....

....

....

....

....

....

....

....

🖤 Parenthood comes with its set of challenges. Share a particularly challenging moment or phase in your parenting journey. How did you navigate it, and what did it teach you?

....

....

....

....

....

....

🖤 If you could describe motherhood in just one word, what would it be?

....

🖤 What's the best piece of advice you received about being a Mom, and from whom?

....

....

....

....

....

....

What's the birth story of each of your children? Did you have any cravings? Were you rushed to the hospital? Were there complications?

♥ Have you experienced a pregnancy loss or an angel baby? How have you dealt with or dealing with the loss?

💗 Reflect on your role as a parent—were you a stay-at-home parent, a single parent, or a working parent? How do you believe this has influenced your parenting style and the relationship with your child(ren)?

....

....

....

....

....

....

....

....

💗 What parts of yourself do you see in your kids?

....

....

....

....

....

....

....

♡ Recall a moment or milestone in your child's life that filled you with immense joy and pride. What made this moment stand out?

....

....

....

....

....

....

♡ What's the greatest gift your children have given you?

....

....

....

....

....

....

....

....

♡ What are the differences between being a parent and a grandparent?

....

....

....

....

....

....

....

♡ As you watched your child step into the role of a parent, what were some changes you noticed in them? Describe your emotions and thoughts as you observed this transition.

....

....

....

....

....

....

....

Describe each of your grandchildren.

What are some characteristics or traits you notice in your grandchildren that remind you of their parents at the same age? Conversely, in what ways are they distinctly their own person? Share your observations and feelings about these similarities and differences.

Your Space: Thoughts and Memories

Need more space? Head to memwah.com.au and record your answers. Don't let a single detail go untold—capture it all on video

In order to write about life, first you must live it.

———————————

Earnest Hemmingway

Culture and Beliefs

Preserving traditions, culture and faith

FAMILY TRADITIONS

Family traditions are the threads that weave the tapestry of family culture, connecting generations. They can be as simple as a Sunday meal together, or as elaborate as annual family reunions.

m Name a family tradition. Briefly describe the tradition.

....
....
....

m How did this tradition begin?

....
....
....

m What does this tradition mean to your family? Why has it continued over the years?

....
....
....

m Detail the steps or activities involved in this tradition.

....
....

m Who is involved in this tradition?

....

How do you define your cultural identity, and what are key aspects that make your culture unique?

How is love traditionally expressed in your culture? Are there any specific customs or practices that symbolize love and care?

In the heart of many families, the kitchen is more than just a place to prepare food; it's where love is expressed and memories are made. Write down your favorite family meal.

Passed down from

Name

Serving

Prep Time

Cook Time

Ingredients

Directions / Method

History of this recipe

💬 What traditions, celebrations, or rituals are important to you and your family?

....

....

....

....

....

....

....

💬 What are common misconceptions or assumptions people have made about you? Have you experienced any form of prejudice or misconceptions, and how have you dealt with it?

....

....

....

....

....

....

....

....

ⓜ What does faith mean to you, and how has this understanding evolved over time?

_____
_____
_____
_____
_____
_____
_____

ⓜ What kinds of spiritual or religious beliefs are important in your family? How have these beliefs shaped your family's traditions and values?

_____
_____
_____
_____
_____
_____
_____

ⓜ What countries or regions do you and your ancestors come from, and what do you know about your family's origins?

....

....

....

....

....

....

ⓜ What were the main reasons your ancestors or your family moved from their original homeland, if they did?

....

....

....

....

....

....

....

....

m Have you ever visited the country or region where your ancestors originated? Or returned back to your original homeland? What was that experience like?

_____

_____

_____

_____

_____

_____

_____

m Are there any family stories or legends that have been passed down through generations?

_____

_____

_____

_____

_____

_____

🅜 What superstitions do you have?

_____
_____
_____
_____
_____
_____

🅜 Which traditions do you hope will continue in our family after you're gone, and why are they important to you?

_____
_____
_____
_____
_____
_____
_____
_____

Your Space: Thoughts and Memories

I still repeat the things you said to me in my head

———————————

Unknown

LOVE LISTS: YOUR TOP 5'S

m Top 5 Music Groups

....

....

m Top 5 Songs

....

....

m Top 5 Movies

....

....

m Top 5 Dishes

....

....

m Top 5 Books

....

....

m Top 5 Sporting Moments

....

....

♡ What's the craziest thing you've ever done in the name of love?

♡ Is it more important to love or be loved?

♡ Worst date story...

What is your love language?

Tell the story of your first love...

Your great love story began when....

_____

_____

_____

_____

_____

_____

_____

_____

_____

_____

_____

_____

_____

_____

_____

Everyone loves a romance! Scan the QR code to record your answer on video with memwah.com.au. Let your loved ones **see** and **hear** the story directly from you.

Tell your engagement story...

🄼 Did you have any cultural or religious differences you had to overcome in your relationship?

....
....
....
....
....
....
....

🄼 Did family chaos ensue on the lead up to the wedding? What happened?

....
....
....
....
....
....
....
....

Describe your wedding day and honeymoon?

What's your love song and what memories does it evoke?

What impact did / does your parents' relationship have on your view of relationships and marriage?

Describe a time when you had your heart broken.

What was the moment you realized that your relationship was no longer the same? Describe your feelings and thoughts during that pivotal time.

Write about the process of coming to terms with the end of your marriage. What were the hardest parts to accept, and how did you eventually find peace?

Share a moment when you faced significant loss or grief. How did this experience change you, and what lessons did you learn about love, life, and resilience in the process?

Grief can manifest in unexpected ways. Share a time when grief surprised you, either by its intensity, its timing, or the form it took. How did you cope with it?

 During times of loss and grief, support systems play a vital role. Who were your pillars of support, and how did they help you through your darkest moments?

💗 What skills do you think you need in order to have a successful relationship?

_____
_____
_____
_____
_____
_____
_____

💗 What qualities do you value the most in a partner, and why are they important?

_____
_____
_____
_____
_____
_____
_____

Now that your children are grown and have families of their own, what are some things you would like to do or achieve for yourself in this next phase of your life? Focus on your personal aspirations and desires. What goals do you want to set.

As we move into different stages of life, such as retirement, and experience changes like friends passing away, how do you plan to stay active, meet new people, and diversify your activities to maintain a fulfilling lifestyle?

As we age, there's a chance one partner may need to care for the other during health challenges. What are some small but meaningful ways you can show appreciation and love to your partner?

What has love taught you about you?

I might be beyond my "Best Before" date, but I'm nowhere near my "Used by" date

---

Val Fell, 93
Australia's oldest university student

Final Reflections

Wisdom for Tomorrow, Letters to the Future

What are your hopes and dreams for your family's future, and how do you envision their lives unfolding?

Can you offer words of wisdom for navigating challenging times or setbacks? Share insights that have guided you through tough moments.

How do you want to be remembered by your loved ones? Reflect on the values and memories you hope to leave behind.

Can you reflect on your happiest moments and what made them special? Share the essence of these memories and why they hold a dear place in your heart.

♥ What's your secret ingredient for a love that lasts? Offer advice on keeping love strong through the years.

♥ What advice would you give regarding pursuing passions and dreams versus choosing a more secure career path? Share your perspective on finding balance.

What's the best money lesson you've learned, and how could it help someone in your family facing financial challenges? Share practical advice or insights.

Thinking back, what's the most important thing you've learned about navigating the ups and downs of a relationship? Share your insights on love and compromise.

Is there someone you'd like to apologise to or seek forgiveness from? What would you say to them if given the chance?

Can you recall a cherished memory or story you'd like to ensure lives on after you're gone? Describe this memory and its significance.

What values or principles do you wish to pass on as your legacy? Reflect on the core beliefs that have shaped your life.

Who has made a significant impact on your life, and what would you like to thank them for? Reflect on the influence they've had on your journey.

Letter 1: Graduating High School

Dear

As you stand on the brink of adulthood, about to graduate high school, I want to tell you...

Letter 2: Entering College/University or Starting a Career

Dear

This new journey you are embarking on—whether it's further education or beginning your career—is filled with opportunities. Here's what I hope you'll discover...

Letter 3: On Your Wedding Day

Dear

Today, as you commit to a life shared with another, remember these words...

Letter 4: Becoming a Parent

Dear

Becoming a parent is one of the most profound changes you will ever experience. As you welcome your own child, here's my advice to you...

Letter 5: Overcoming Challenges

Dear

Life is full of ups and downs. During those times when you face challenges, I hope you remember...

Letter 6: Following Your Dreams

Dear

Pursuing your dreams is a journey that requires courage, resilience, and heart. As you chase what truly matters to you, always keep in mind...

Have you thought about your final resting place and the type of ceremony you'd prefer? Share any specific wishes you have for your burial or memorial service.

Is there a poem, song, hymn, reading, or piece of scripture that resonates with you or captures your philosophy on life? Which words would you choose to be shared in your memory, and why?

If this were your final goodbye, what message would you want your loved ones to hold onto? Share your parting words of love and wisdom.

Make it unforgettable: Use the QR code for a free 2-minute story recording on Memwah.com.au. Share your heartfelt message for a lasting memory.

& *m*

Your Own Questions, Notes or Photos

HANDY DIARY
FOR
1931

To order this Diary give Number stamped on cover.

Printed in Great Britain for
COLLINS BROS. & CO., LTD.
MENTMORE AVENUE, ROSEBERY,
SYDNEY.
Branches—Melbourne, Brisbane and Perth.

THANK YOU

As you come to the end of this journal, we invite you to pause and reflect on the experience of chronicling your life's story.

What was it like for you to navigate through the pages of your past, to revisit memories, and to articulate your hopes, dreams, and lessons learned? How has this process of reflection impacted your view of your life's journey?

_____

_____

_____

_____

_____

_____

_____

_____

_____

_____

_____

_____

SPREAD THE WORD

We, the team at Memwah, want to extend our heartfelt thanks for embarking on this deeply personal journey with us. Your courage in sharing your story is a gift—not only to those closest to you but to future generations who will seek to know where they came from and the stories that shaped their heritage.

We encourage you to take the next step in preserving your legacy by visiting our website at www.memwah.com.au. Explore how you can further bring your stories to life by recording them on video. It's a powerful way to connect with loved ones, sharing your voice, expressions, and emotions in a way that written words alone cannot capture.

Lastly, we invite you to **leave a review of your experience.** By sharing your thoughts, you become part of a growing community dedicated to capturing and preserving stories. Your feedback not only supports us in enhancing this journey for others but also encourages more individuals to document their stories. In a world where every story matters, your review can inspire confidence in someone else contemplating whether to share theirs.

Remember:

Your story is a vital thread in the fabric of history. Let's work together to capture a generation of stories before it's too late. Your legacy, your lessons, and your life are invaluable treasures to be cherished for years to come.

Scan to leave a review so others can capture their story

www.ingramcontent.com/pod-product-compliance
Lightning Source LLC
Chambersburg PA
CBHW052146070526
44585CB00017B/2003